Wings

MORE THAN 50 HIGH-FLYING RECIPES FOR AMERICA'S FAVORITE SNACK

Wings

MORE THAN **50**
HIGH-FLYING RECIPES
FOR AMERICA'S
FAVORITE SNACK

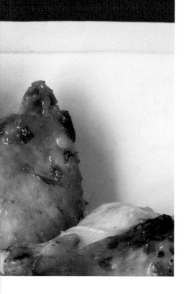

Wings

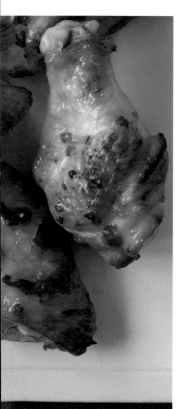

Debbie Moose

PHOTOGRAPHY BY JASON WYCHE

WILEY

JOHN WILEY & SONS, INC.

Published by John Wiley & Sons, Inc., Hoboken, New Jersey
Published simultaneously in Canada

For general information on our other products and services or for technical support, please contact our Customer Care Department within the United States at (800) 762-2974, outside the United States at (317) 572-3993 or fax (317) 572-4002.

Wiley also publishes its books in a variety of electronic formats. Some content that appears in print may not be available in electronic books.
For more information about Wiley products, visit our web site at www.wiley.com.

BOOK DESIGN BY DEBORAH KERNER
PROP STYLING BY LESLIE SIEGEL
FOOD STYLING BY ALISON ATTENBOROUGH

Library of Congress Cataloging-in-Publication Data:
Moose, Debbie.
    Wings : More than 50 high-flying recipes for America's favorite snack / Debbie Moose.
        p. cm.
    Includes index.
ISBN 978-0-470-28347-9 (cloth : acid-free)
1. Cookery (Chicken) I. Title.
TX750.5.C45M66 2009
641.6'65—dc22
2008012191

Printed in China

10 9 8 7 6 5 4 3 2 1

To Rob,

as always,

for twenty-six years

of winging it

CONTENTS

Takeoff 11

The fundamentals of wing preparation, including things you'll
need to know to safely handle and cook poultry. It's easy
to cut up the wings yourself, and you'll learn how here.

Gliding 15

Even a rookie can make great wings with these recipes. Quick
and simple rubs and marinades, using few ingredients, get the
action moving. Look here for basic grilled, fried, and roasted
wings to which you can add your own embellishments.

Fire It Up 47

Got that burning desire? Satisfy it by bringing on the heat, with everything from the hottest habanero to blazing black pepper, from Cajun spice to sizzling Mexican flavors. And don't forget the classic Buffalo Wings that started the madness.

Fly High 81

Welcome to the big leagues. Wings jet around the world with these exotic seasonings. Try wings with a sassy Thai touch or Chinese five-spice flavor.

Dressed to Thrill 117

Sauces, dips, salsas, and a few surprises to spice up your wings.

Acknowledgments

I thank all the recipe tasters who stepped
up to the plate in this effort:

Anthony Nance, Shelley Kramer, and the other stylists
and clients of the Elan Group

My husband's coworkers at Scenera

The *News & Observer* (Raleigh, North Carolina)
features department

My sister-in-law Carol Vatz and her coworkers at
A.B. Combs Elementary School

The members of Joshinkan Aikido Dojo

The hungry interns and staff of Interact

I also thank Jim Crabtree, Denise Rhodes, Dean McCord,
Peggy Dennis, Kathy Hedberg, Elizabeth Karmel,
Lucy Saunders, Judith Fertig, and Karen Adler
for their contributions.

Thanks also to my agent, Carla Glasser,
for her excellent advice and support.

Takeoff

It's third and long, ten seconds to go in the fourth quarter, two laps to the checkered flag. A rumble hits the pit of your stomach. What happens when sports fans get hungry? They grab a fistful of juicy wings, which carry them through until the score is settled.

It was a great day in snacking history when the Buffalo wing was invented at Buffalo, New York's Anchor Bar. Until that fateful day, those caught up in passion for their sport had to make do with boring chips and dip or stale pretzels. Poor fuel for the true sports lover. Then the sports bar arose, and wings were lifted along with it. (Or could it have been the other way around?) Today, wherever you find fans gathered together, you will find a plate of wings nearby, ready to sustain them on the path to glory.

Why wings? Those who watch great athletes must think like great athletes, if they take their viewing seriously. You don't want to get filled up with heavy food, which would weigh you down when jumping up to celebrate a great drive to the basket or an awesome tackle. But you need a little protein in your system to ride out those four-hour stock car races and to balance out the libations that typically accompany the events.

The biggest time of year for wings, according to the National Chicken Council, is Super Bowl weekend, when football fans consume more than one billion of them.

The best thing about wings is the taste. They pack more tender flavor into a smaller package than almost any other food.

If you order expensive wings at a bar, you may be disappointed. Fans often end up with greasy variations on the Buffalo wing theme and flavor choices limited to hot, flaming, and nuclear.

Wings can be so much more. It's time for them to soar with flavors that let their goodness shine through. Grilling, roasting, or frying them at home will give you wings worthy of a championship ring.

I'll give you easy directions for basic techniques. Quick, time-saving recipes in Gliding will let you get to the eating action fast. In Fly High, I'll explore ingredients from around the world along with dipping sauces, dressings, marinades, and rubs that will expand your range. You'll be the envy of other fans who are stuck with pitiful piles of pasty poultry. And, of course, I'll pay homage to the snack's roots with spicy flavors in Fire It Up. Dressed to Thrill offers sauces and dips to mix and match with your favorite wings.

There are so many options that you'll start thinking of wings not just as munchies but as cocktail party hors d'ouvres or tapas-style dishes for lunch or dinner.

. Step to the fowl line with any of these recipes and you'll be a winner.

THE FUNDAMENTALS

A whole wing comes in three clearly defined parts: the "drumette," which looks like a miniature drumstick; the piece with two small bones, called the flat; and the pointy tip, called the flapper.

You can purchase already-cut-up wings, but you save a little money by doing the work yourself. It's not difficult, though a very sharp knife is helpful. Bend the joint between the drumette and the flat backward to loosen the joint. Cut the two pieces apart where the knife easily slips into the joint. Then, cut off the flapper. But don't throw those tips away—save them in a bag in the freezer for making chicken stock.

You could also use a sharp pair of kitchen shears instead of a knife to dissect the wings.

I've noticed that some people are picky about their wings and have great disdain for the flat. If you're one of those folks, or are cooking for them, you'd be better off purchasing packages of just drumettes, which are easily available.

As soon as you finish cutting apart the wings, immediately clean the cutting board, knife or shears, and any surface that has touched raw poultry (your hands, too) with hot, soapy water. Do not use the same items for preparing any other ingredients until they have been thoroughly cleaned. Why? It's called cross contamination, folks, and it can ruin a party faster than a call to the cops.

For the same reason, never use marinade that has held raw poultry to baste wings as they cook. If you want to baste, make a second batch of the marinade strictly for that purpose. Throw away that used marinade.

Since we've opened the food safety playbook, here are some other points to remember. Frozen wings should be thawed in the refrigerator, in cold water, or in the microwave, never left on the kitchen counter. They should thaw within three to nine hours in the 'fridge. To thaw wings in cold water, place them in a watertight plastic bag and immerse them. Change the water every 30 minutes or so. This process will probably take two hours. Thawing times in the microwave will vary depending on the number of wings.

No matter how you prepare the wings, make sure they are completely cooked. At the end of the minimum suggested cooking time for each recipe, cut into the thickest meat, near the bone, with the tip of a sharp knife. You should not see any pink or red, but only clear juices. An instant-read thermometer should read 170°F, but it can be difficult to fit a probe into the small wings. The knife-test method works well.

GAME TIME

In this book, I offer a variety of ways to flavor your wings. You can use marinades, rubs, sauces, or glazes. Or you can cook the wings simply—following my basic frying, grilling, and roasting methods—and offer an array of dips and dressings. The first method offers deeper and more unusual flavors and combinations. The second approach is an easy way to accommodate a crowd that includes both fans of hot food and those who shun it. Tailor your plan to the team you're feeding.

I would probably eat a basketball if it were cooked on a grill, I love grilled food so much. But in some cases, you might want to roast your wings. Most of the recipes in this book that are roasted in the oven can also be prepared on the grill for a crispier texture, or if you just like the grilled flavor. The grilled wings can be roasted indoors, although they'll lack that special crunch. Just follow the basic grilling or roasting directions if switching techniques. I will note any concerns with switching cooking methods in the individual recipes.

All wings taste best served right after they're cooked. If you must prepare them ahead and reheat, do it in a 300°F oven instead of the microwave to preserve the texture.

GLIDING

BFW
(Basic Fried Wings)

▶ Crunchy and classic, these deep-fried fliers are what most folks think of when they think wings.

Vegetable oil
1½ cups all-purpose flour
1½ teaspoons freshly ground black pepper
1½ teaspoons salt
1 teaspoon paprika
¾ teaspoon cayenne pepper (optional)
12 wings, cut in half at joints, wing tips removed and discarded

Pour enough vegetable oil into a heavy saucepan to hold the wings and allow them to float. Attach a frying thermometer to the pot (or use an electric frying pan or deep fryer). Heat the oil over medium-high heat until it reaches 360°F.

Meanwhile, combine the flour, black pepper, salt, paprika, and cayenne, if using, in a large bowl. Dredge the wings in the mixture and shake off any excess.

When the oil is hot, use tongs to gently lower the wings into the oil. Do not crowd them; they should float freely. You will need to cook the wings in batches.

Monitor the oil temperature carefully and adjust the heat up or down to keep it near 360°F.

continues on p. 18

Cook the wings for 10 to 12 minutes, or until they float to the top of the oil and are golden brown.

Drain the wings on a wire rack placed over a plate, then serve with your favorite dip.

BRW
(Basic
Roasted Wings)

▶ The classic oven-cooked version of the wing, ready for sauces and sides of all kinds.

12 wings, cut in half
　at joints, wing tips
　removed and discarded
Olive oil
Salt
Freshly ground black
　pepper

Preheat the oven to 350°F. Cover a rimmed baking sheet with foil and spray the foil with nonstick cooking spray. Lightly rub each wing with olive oil and place on the baking sheet. Sprinkle with salt and pepper. Roast for 35 to 40 minutes or until done.

Serve with your favorite dip or sauce.

BGW (Basic Grilled Wings)

▶ Grilling may be the best way for wings to shine, because they become flavorful bites of smoky goodness. Dress them up with sauces or dips.

12 wings, cut in half at joints, wing tips removed and discarded
Olive oil
Salt
Freshly ground black pepper

Prepare a gas or charcoal grill for direct cooking. Rub the wings lightly with olive oil and sprinkle with salt and pepper to taste.

Place the wings on the grill and cook, turning frequently, for 15 to 20 minutes or until done.

Crispy Italian Fliers

▶ Give your snack time an Italian accent with these herb-flavored treats. To make finely ground cornmeal, simply grind regular cornmeal in a food processor for a few seconds. Use your favorite marinara sauce for dipping, if you like.

1 cup all-purpose flour
½ cup finely ground
    white cornmeal
1½ tablespoons grated
    Parmesan
2 teaspoons dried
    oregano
1 teaspoon dried thyme,
    lightly crushed
½ teaspoon dried basil
½ teaspoon garlic powder
½ teaspoon salt
½ teaspoon freshly
    ground black pepper
12 wings, cut in half
    at joints, wing tips
    removed and discarded
Vegetable oil
Warm marinara sauce
    (optional)

In a large bowl, combine flour, cornmeal, Parmesan, oregano, thyme, basil, garlic powder, salt, and pepper. Coat the wings in the mixture and shake off any excess.

Pour about 1 inch of vegetable oil into a frying pan and heat to 350°F. Fry the wings for 5 to 6 minutes on each side, or until golden brown. You may need to turn frequently near the end for even browning. Drain the wings on a rack set over a platter.

Serve the wings with warm marinara sauce for dipping, if desired.

Easy Holiday Party Wings

▶ These wings made their debut at a Christmas party, and those bad boys and girls left none for Santa. Briefly baking the chicken removes some of the fat. But after that, this recipe is toss-it-in-the-slow-cooker easy! Increase the cayenne if you like it hotter.

18 wings, cut in half at joints, wing tips removed and discarded
1 cup hoisin sauce
1 cup apricot preserves
1 teaspoon dry mustard
4 cloves garlic, chopped
2 tablespoons orange juice
¼ teaspoon cayenne pepper

Preheat the oven to 350°F. Cover a rimmed baking sheet with foil and spray the foil with nonstick cooking spray. Place the wings on the baking sheet and bake for 20 minutes.

In a slow cooker, combine the hoisin sauce, apricot preserves, dry mustard, chopped garlic, orange juice, and cayenne; stir well to combine.

Remove the wings from the baking sheet with tongs, letting any juice drain away, then place the wings in the slow cooker. Toss to coat the wings with the sauce.

Cook on the Low heat setting for 3 to 4 hours or on High for 2 hours.

Faux Fryers

▶ All the flavor of Southern-style fried wings without the oil-spattered kitchen. If you make these ahead of time, reheat them on a baking sheet in a 300°F oven to revive their crispness—don't use the microwave.

12 wings, cut in half at joints, wing tips removed and discarded

2 cups buttermilk

5 cups coarsely crushed corn flakes

4 teaspoons dried thyme

2 teaspoons dried basil

1 teaspoon salt

1 teaspoon freshly ground black pepper

Place the wings in a resealable plastic bag and pour in the buttermilk. Refrigerate for 2 to 3 hours.

Preheat the oven to 400°F. Cover a rimmed baking sheet with foil and spray the foil with nonstick cooking spray.

Drain the wings, but do not rinse them. In a large bowl, combine the crushed corn flakes, thyme, basil, salt, and pepper. Roll the wings in the mixture, pressing it in lightly to cover. Place the wings on the baking sheet.

Bake for 40 to 45 minutes or until done.

Wings
à la Aunt Ida

▶ My husband's aunt Ida marinated her Thanksgiving turkey in a mixture of, believe it or not, cola and orange juice. It was always delicious, so I figured it would work for wings, too! Don't use diet soda—the sugar is important.

12 wings, cut in half at joints, wing tips removed and discarded
1 cup cola
1 cup orange juice
1 teaspoon garlic powder
½ teaspoon onion powder
4 teaspoons paprika
½ teaspoon salt
1 teaspoon freshly ground black pepper

Place the wings in a reclosable plastic bag. In a small bowl, combine the cola and orange juice. Pour the mixture into the bag and refrigerate for 8 hours or overnight.

Preheat the oven to 350°F. Cover a rimmed baking sheet with foil and spray the foil with nonstick cooking spray. Remove the wings from the marinade and place them on the prepared baking sheet. Discard the marinade.

Combine the garlic powder, onion powder, paprika, salt, and pepper. Sprinkle half of the mixture over the wings, then turn the wings over and sprinkle on the rest.

Bake for 20 to 30 minutes or until done.

Down on the Spicy Chicken Ranch

▶ Round up those hungry fans and feed them fast with this recipe. "My kids would love these!" one of my tasters said. If you switch to the grill, watch these wings carefully to avoid burning the rub.

2 tablespoons ranch salad
  dressing mix
2 teaspoons chili powder
1 teaspoon paprika
6 tablespoons olive oil
12 wings, cut in half
  at joints, wing tips
  removed and discarded

Preheat the oven to 400°F. Cover a rimmed baking sheet with foil and spray the foil with nonstick cooking spray.

In a small bowl, combine the dressing mix, chili powder, and paprika. Pour the olive oil into a small bowl.

Dip each wing in the olive oil and let the excess drip off, then place wings on the prepared baking sheet. Sprinkle the dressing mixture over the wings and let sit for 20 minutes.

Bake for 30 minutes or until done.

Mighty Mustard Wings

▶ In South Carolina, pork barbecue is served with a thick mustard sauce. Turns out, it's great for wings, too. Stash them in the slow cooker and you'll have no distractions from your party guests or the big game.

8 tablespoons (1 stick) butter
4 cups yellow mustard
2 cups apple cider vinegar
2 teaspoons onion powder
A few shakes of hot pepper sauce
Salt and freshly ground black pepper to taste
12 wings, cut in half at joints, wing tips removed and discarded

Melt the butter in a saucepan over medium heat. Stir in the mustard, apple cider vinegar, onion powder, hot pepper sauce, salt, and pepper. Reduce the heat to medium-low and simmer, stirring, until thick, 5 to 6 minutes. Cover the sauce and refrigerate overnight to let the flavors blend.

Preheat the oven to 350°F. Cover a rimmed baking sheet with foil and spray the foil with nonstick cooking spray. Place the wings on the baking sheet and bake for 20 minutes.

Remove the wings from the baking sheet with tongs, letting any juice drain away, then place the wings in the slow cooker. Add the sauce, and toss to coat the wings.

Cook on the Low heat setting for 3 to 4 hours or on High for 2 hours.

When Pigs Fly

▶ At my gym, we talk about food a lot. One day, a guy named Wayne told me about a chicken recipe he picked up from another gym denizen. He assured me it was a healthy recipe, but he couldn't remember all the ingredients (his wife does the cooking). As I walked the indoor track, Wayne flagged me down and introduced me to a woman on a step machine: the source of the chicken recipe, Peggy Dennis. When Peggy described the recipe, I couldn't believe the ingredients. You'll be skeptical, too, but these are great wings. As for healthy eating: "Butter is all natural," Peggy says. I've made a few changes to Peggy's original recipe to adapt it to wings (she uses chicken parts). Don't cook these on the grill.

3 cups pork rinds

2 large eggs

4 tablespoons butter, melted and slightly cooled

12 wings, cut in half at joints, wing tips removed and discarded

Preheat the oven to 400°F. Cover a rimmed baking sheet with foil and spray the foil with nonstick cooking spray.

Place the pork rinds in a heavy plastic bag and seal. Roll with a rolling pin or crush the bag with your hands until the rinds become coarse crumbs (do not crush them too finely).

Lightly beat the eggs into the melted butter. Place the crushed pork rinds on a plate. Dip the wings into the egg-butter

continues on p. 34

mixture and let the excess drip off. Roll the wings in the crushed pork rinds, pressing lightly to help them adhere to the meat, and place the wings on the baking sheet.

Roast for 30 minutes or until done. Serve warm.

Cheery BBQ Wings

▶ I spent several years in Salisbury, North Carolina, the home of Cheerwine. There, folks use the soft drink for everything from cakes to gelatin molds. It's a great base for a sweet-spicy barbecue sauce, too. If you can't find Cheerwine, use a similar cherry-cola flavored soda.

12 wings, cut in half
  at joints, wing tips
  removed and discarded
3 cups Cheerwine
½ cup tomato paste
½ cup white vinegar
2 tablespoons plus
  2 teaspoons
  Worcestershire sauce
2 tablespoons plus 2
  teaspoons molasses
1½ teaspoons crushed red
  pepper
½ teaspoon cayenne
  pepper
¼ teaspoon salt or to taste
1 teaspoon freshly ground
  black pepper or to taste

Preheat the oven to 350°F. Cover a rimmed baking sheet with foil and spray with cooking spray. Place the wings on the baking sheet and cook for 20 minutes.

In a large saucepan, combine the Cheerwine, tomato paste, vinegar, Worcestershire sauce, molasses, crushed red pepper, cayenne, salt, and black pepper. Bring the mixture to a boil, stirring, over medium-high heat, then reduce the heat to a simmer and cook until slightly thickened, 3 to 4 minutes.

Place the wings in the pot of a slow cooker. Pour the sauce over the wings and stir to coat. Cover and cook on the High setting for 2 hours or on Low for 4 hours.

Note: The sauce can be made and refrigerated two to three days ahead of time. Make an extra batch to use as a dipping sauce for plain grilled or roasted wings.

Crunchy Lemon-Pepper Wings

▶ My tasters liked these because they have a ton of zingy flavor without the bite of hot wings. The pepper also makes a crunchy coating.

¼ cup lemon pepper
    seasoning
2 tablespoons chopped
    fresh chives
3 to 4 tablespoons olive
    oil
12 wings, cut in half
    at joints, wing tips
    removed and discarded

On a plate, combine the lemon pepper and chives. Pour the olive oil in a separate small bowl. Dip the wings lightly in the olive oil, then roll in the lemon pepper mixture. Let the coated wings sit for about 15 minutes.

Prepare a gas or charcoal grill for direct cooking. Place the wings on the grill and cook, turning frequently, for 15 to 20 minutes or until done. Watch carefully and adjust the heat to avoid burning the coating.

Wings with Rob's Barbecue Sauce

▶ My husband has made this barbecue sauce for years, and it's great on all cuts of poultry. Margarine works better than butter in this concoction. The sauce is not ideal for the grill, so let's keep these in the oven.

1 sliced onion
8 tablespoons (1 stick) margarine
½ cup ketchup
¼ cup white wine vinegar
2 tablespoons sugar
2 tablespoons Worcestershire sauce
1 tablespoon Dijon mustard
1½ teaspoons salt
½ teaspoon freshly ground black pepper
¼ teaspoon cayenne pepper
1 thick slice of lemon
12 wings, cut in half at joints, wing tips removed and discarded

Preheat the oven to 350°F.

In a large saucepan, combine the onion, margarine, ketchup, vinegar, sugar, Worcestershire, Dijon mustard, salt, black pepper, cayenne, and lemon. Heat, stirring, over medium heat until the margarine is melted and all the ingredients are combined.

Place the wings in a baking dish and pour the sauce over them. Cover and cook for 15 minutes, then uncover and cook 10 to 15 minutes or until done.

Crunchy Onion Wings

▶ You know those canned fried onions that make an appearance in the green bean casserole every Thanksgiving (now, don't deny that you serve it; I know you do). They make a great, easy crust for roasted wings, too. The coating may burn on the grill, so avoid that method.

2½ (2.8 ounce) cans fried
   onions
¾ teaspoon garlic powder
1 large egg
12 wings, cut in half
   at joints, wing tips
   removed and discarded

Preheat the oven to 400°F. Cover a rimmed baking sheet with foil and spray the foil with nonstick cooking spray.

Pour the fried onions into a shallow bowl and crush with your hands to break up any large pieces. Stir in the garlic powder.

In another small bowl, lightly beat the egg. Dip each wing into the egg, then roll in the fried onion mixture, pressing to make the mixture stick to the wing. Place the wings on the baking sheet. Bake for 25 to 30 minutes or until done. Turn the wings over about halfway through the cooking time.

Flying Down By the Bay

▶ Who says Old Bay seasoning is just for seafood? It plays well with wings, too, with plenty of flavor but not a lot of heat.

4 teaspoons fresh lemon juice

⅓ cup olive oil

2 teaspoons apple cider vinegar

2 tablespoons Old Bay seasoning

12 wings, cut in half at joints, wing tips removed and discarded

Combine the lemon juice, olive oil, vinegar, and Old Bay in a small bowl.

Place the wings in a resealable plastic bag. Pour the mixture over the wings and shake the bag to coat them. Refrigerate for 2 hours or as long as overnight.

Preheat the oven to 400°F. Cover a rimmed baking sheet with foil and spray the foil with nonstick cooking spray.

Remove the wings from the marinade and place them on the prepared baking sheet. Discard the marinade. Bake for 25 to 30 minutes or until done.

Curry in a Hurry Wings

▶ Flavorful but not hot, these wings use ingredients easily found in the supermarket.

2 cups plain yogurt
3 tablespoons curry powder
2 tablespoons vegetable oil
2 teaspoons ground cinnamon
1 tablespoon plus 1 teaspoon chopped garlic
1 teaspoon salt
12 wings, cut in half at joints, wing tips removed and discarded

In a bowl, combine the yogurt, curry powder, oil, cinnamon, garlic, and salt. Place the wings in a resealable plastic bag. Pour in the yogurt mixture and shake to cover the wings. Refrigerate for 2 hours or as long as overnight.

Preheat the oven to 400°F. Cover a rimmed baking sheet with foil and spray the foil with nonstick cooking spray. Remove the wings from the marinade, letting the marinade drip off. Place the wings on the baking sheet. Discard the marinade. Roast for 20 to 25 minutes or until done.

Super Simple Fan Feeders

▶ I tossed these wings together for the Super Bowl, and their teriyaki-like flavor scored a touchdown! Keep frozen pure lemon juice on hand for quick marinades like this one. Grilling really brings out the flavor, but these wings would do fine in the oven, too.

⅔ cup fresh lemon juice
4 tablespoons soy sauce
2 tablespoons sugar
1½ teaspoons garlic powder
½ teaspoon onion powder
12 wings, cut in half at joints, wing tips removed and discarded

In a bowl, combine the lemon juice, soy sauce, sugar, garlic powder and onion powder. Stir to dissolve the sugar.

Place the wings in a resealable plastic bag. Pour the lemon juice mixture into the bag, close the bag, and shake to coat the wings. Refrigerate for 2 hours or as long as overnight.

Prepare a gas or charcoal grill for direct cooking. Place the wings on the grill and cook, turning frequently, for 15 to 20 minutes or until done.

Nice Spice Wings

▶ You can throw these sweet, spicy, and mysterious wings together in a minute, using items from your well-stocked spice rack. Feel free to omit the cayenne pepper if you want a milder flavor, although these are not extremely hot. If you grill these wings, turn them frequently or use indirect heat to prevent the rub from burning.

2 tablespoons ground cinnamon
2 teaspoons turmeric
2 teaspoons light brown sugar
1 teaspoon salt
1 teaspoon garlic powder
½ teaspoon onion powder
½ teaspoon cayenne pepper
½ teaspoon freshly ground black pepper
12 wings, cut in half at joints, wing tips removed and discarded

In a bowl, combine the cinnamon, turmeric, brown sugar, salt, garlic powder, onion powder, cayenne, and black pepper. Stir well, eliminating any clumps. Place the wings in a resealable plastic bag. Pour the rub into the bag, close the bag, and shake it well until all the wings are coated.

Preheat the oven to 400°F. Cover a rimmed baking sheet with foil and spray the foil with nonstick cooking spray. Place the wings on the baking sheet and let them sit for 15 to 20 minutes. Roast for 20 to 25 minutes or until done.

FIRE IT UP

Where There's Smoke, There's Paprika

▶ Smoked paprika has a great woody flavor. I love it on everything from deviled eggs to simple roasted chicken. Pairing it with cayenne really kicks it.

3 tablespoons smoked
   paprika
1 teaspoon light brown
   sugar
¾ teaspoon cayenne
   pepper
½ teaspoon salt
¾ teaspoon freshly
   ground black pepper
½ teaspoon ground
   allspice
¼ teaspoon ground cloves
12 wings, cut in half
   at joints, wing tips
   removed and discarded

In a small bowl, combine the smoked paprika, sugar, cayenne, salt, black pepper, ground allspice, and ground cloves.

Cover a rimmed baking sheet with foil and spray the foil with nonstick cooking spray. Rub the wings liberally with the spice mixture and place them on the baking sheet. Let sit for 20 minutes.

Meanwhile, preheat the oven to 350°F. Bake the wings for 30 minutes, or until done.

Quick Caffeinated Wings

▶ Forget your cup of coffee this morning? Try these wings, which include instant espresso and the bite of peppery steak seasoning. It's heat of a different color. If cooking these on the grill, turn them frequently and lower the heat to prevent burning.

¼ cup black pepper–based steak seasoning (such as McCormick's Grill Mates)
3 tablespoons instant espresso
3 tablespoons light brown sugar
⅓ cup olive oil
12 wings, cut in half at joints, wing tips removed and discarded

In a small bowl, combine the steak seasoning, instant espresso, and brown sugar.

Cover a rimmed baking sheet with foil and spray the foil with nonstick cooking spray. Rub the wings lightly with the olive oil, then rub liberally with the spice mixture. Place them on the baking sheet. Let sit for 20 minutes.

Preheat the oven to 400°F. Bake the wings for 20 minutes, or until done.

Wait-for-It Fiery Fiends

▶ You won't think these wings are hot at first. After a minute, you'll know that the world's hottest pepper is in their marinade. Don't say you weren't warned. Up the heat, if you dare, by making a second batch of the marinade to use as a dipping sauce. Never reuse marinade that has held raw meat.

¼ cup olive oil
1 small onion, coarsely chopped
3 tablespoons chopped garlic
2 tablespoons sherry vinegar
1 habanero chile, quartered
2 teaspoons salt
½ teaspoon freshly ground black pepper
1 cup chopped fresh parsley
12 wings, cut in half at joints, wing tips removed and discarded

Place the olive oil, onion, garlic, vinegar, habanero, salt, and black pepper in the bowl of a food processor fitted with the chopping blade. Process briefly, until the mixture becomes a chunky paste. Add the parsley and pulse just to blend.

Place the wings in a resealable plastic bag. Pour in the paste, seal, and toss to coat well. Refrigerate for 8 hours or overnight.

Prepare a gas or charcoal grill for direct cooking. Remove the wings from the marinade and discard the marinade. Place the wings on the grill and cook, turning frequently, for 15 to 20 minutes or until done.

Sneaky Smokies

▶ The smoky flavor of the chipotles (which are actually smoked jalapeños) creeps up on you, and next thing you know, you're hit with the heat. Ahhh.

½ cup chipotle hot sauce
(such as Tabasco
Chipotle)
¼ cup orange juice
2 teaspoons cider vinegar
¼ teaspoon cayenne
pepper
½ teaspoon chopped
garlic
12 wings, cut in half
at joints, wing tips
removed and discarded

In a small bowl, combine the hot sauce, orange juice, cider vinegar, cayenne, and garlic. Put the wings in a reclosable plastic bag. Pour in the hot sauce mixture and refrigerate for 8 hours or overnight.

Preheat the oven to 400°F. Cover a rimmed baking sheet with foil and spray the foil with nonstick cooking spray. Remove the wings from the marinade and place them on the prepared baking sheet. Discard the marinade.

Bake 30 to 40 minutes or until done.

Spicy Brown-Ale Brined Wings

▶ My beer buddy Lucy Saunders says these goodies are hotter than a Stanley Cup playoff, so consider yourself warned. The recipe is from her great cookbook *Grilling With Beer: Bastes, BBQ Sauces, Mops, Marinades and More, Made with Craft Beer* (F&B Communications, 2006). And there's more at www.grillingwithbeer.com. Keep these on the grill for best results.

24 ounces brown ale

½ cup light brown sugar

½ cup kosher salt

5 pounds wings, cut in half at joints, wing tips removed and discarded

1 cup (2 sticks) butter

¼ cup minced fresh jalapeños

2 tablespoons minced garlic

½ cup hot pepper sauce, or more to taste

½ cup Sriracha or Asian sweet-hot chile sauce

1 teaspoon finely ground black pepper

Pinch ground cinnamon

2 tablespoons black or toasted sesame seeds (optional garnish)

In a large bowl, combine the ale, brown sugar, and salt and whisk until the sugar and salt are dissolved. Place the wings in the bowl and stir to coat. Cover and refrigerate for 4 to 8 hours.

In a large skillet over low heat, melt the butter, then add the jalapeños and garlic. Cook, stirring, until the jalapeños are tender, 3 to 4 minutes. Add the hot pepper sauce, Sriracha, pepper, and cinnamon. Mix well and simmer for 3 minutes. Place in a blender and puree until smooth. Set aside.

Prepare a gas or charcoal grill for indirect cooking. Soak 24 (10-inch) bamboo skewers in water for 20 to 30 minutes.

Alternatively, place a grill basket on the grill to heat.

Drain the wings; discard the brine. Thread the wings on the soaked skewers, keeping pieces of similar sizes together so that the chicken will cook evenly. Place the skewers on the grill or the wings on the grill basket. Cook the wings for 25 minutes, turning every 5 minutes, until very brown and crispy.

Place the cooked wings on a platter and drizzle with the Sriracha mixture. Sprinkle with sesame seeds, if using.

Taco Time Grillers

▶ Using prepared taco-seasoning mix makes these wings a breeze to throw together. Use reduced-salt seasoning, if available. This snack is plenty spicy, but add the cayenne if you want to light more fire.

1 tablespoon plus 2
  teaspoons taco-
  seasoning mix
¼ cup fresh lime juice
1 teaspoon chili powder
Dash or two of cayenne
  pepper (optional)
12 wings, cut in half
  at joints, wing tips
  removed and discarded

In a small bowl, stir together the taco-seasoning mix, lime juice, chili powder, and cayenne, if using. Toss the wings in the mixture until they are coated.

Prepare a gas or charcoal grill for direct cooking. Place the wings on the grill and cook, turning frequently, for 15 to 20 minutes or until done.

Having
a Heat Wave

▶ This recipe is a tropical blast from the Caribbean. A fruity, habanero-based hot sauce, not a vinegar-based one, is the best choice for this dish.

1¼ cups orange juice

Juice of 2 limes

⅓ cup fruity Caribbean-style hot sauce

2 tablespoons dried basil

2 tablespoons dried thyme

1 tablespoon dried marjoram

1 teaspoon dry mustard

1 cup chopped fresh parsley

12 wings, cut in half at joints, wing tips removed and discarded

In a small bowl, combine the orange juice, lime juice, hot sauce, basil, thyme, marjoram, and dry mustard. Mix thoroughly, then stir in the parsley.

Place the wings in a reclosable plastic bag. Pour in the juice mixture. Refrigerate for 8 hours or overnight.

Prepare a gas or charcoal grill for direct cooking. Remove the wings from the marinade and discard the marinade. Cook the wings, turning frequently, for 15 to 20 minutes or until done.

Classic Buffalo Wings

▶ The wings that started it all were born at the Anchor Bar in Buffalo, New York. There are many similar versions of the sauce. To make the recipe even simpler, you can purchase frozen fried wings, but the ones you make yourself taste much better! And you can wrap and freeze the cooked wings so they'll be ready for any occasion.

Vegetable oil for deep
   frying
1½ cups all-purpose flour
1½ teaspoons freshly
   ground black pepper
1½ teaspoons salt
1 teaspoon paprika
¾ teaspoon cayenne
   pepper (optional)
12 wings, cut in half
   at joints, wing tips
   removed and discarded
4 tablespoons (½ stick)
   butter
⅓ cup vinegar-based hot
   sauce

Pour enough vegetable oil into a heavy saucepan to hold the wings and allow them to float. Attach a frying thermometer to the pot (or use an electric frying pan or deep fryer). Heat the oil over medium-high heat until it reaches 360°F.

Meanwhile, combine the flour, black pepper, salt, paprika, and cayenne, if using, in a large bowl. Dredge the wings in the mixture and shake off any excess.

When the oil is hot, use tongs to gently lower the wings into the oil. Do not crowd them; they should float freely. You will need to cook the wings in batches.

continues on p. 61

Monitor the oil temperature carefully and adjust the heat up or down to keep it near 360°F. Cook the wings for 10 to 12 minutes, or until they float to the top of the oil and are golden brown.

Drain the wings on a wire rack placed over a plate, then place in a large bowl.

In a medium saucepan over medium heat, melt the butter. Stir in the hot sauce. Pour the sauce over the wings and toss to coat.

Tangy Thai Wings

▶ The flavors of fresh ginger and hot Thai chili-garlic sauce carry these wings to an exotic locale. The heat builds as you eat them, so watch out.

¼ cup vegetable oil
¼ cup fresh lime juice
3 tablespoons Thai chili-garlic sauce
2 tablespoons soy sauce
1 teaspoon grated fresh ginger
1 tablespoon chopped garlic
2 teaspoons honey
12 wings, cut in half at joints, wing tips removed and discarded

Combine the oil, lime juice, garlic sauce, soy sauce, ginger, garlic, and honey in a bowl and stir until the honey is dissolved.

Place the wings in a resealable plastic bag. Pour the ginger mixture over the wings and shake to coat. Refrigerate for 2 hours or as long as overnight.

Preheat the oven to 400°F. Cover a rimmed baking sheet with foil and spray the foil with nonstick cooking spray.

Remove the wings from the marinade and discard the marinade. Place the wings on the baking sheet. Bake for 25 to 30 minutes or until done.

Buffaloes of a Different Color

▶ Buffalo wings don't have to be red. The new green hot pepper sauces, which use green jalapeños, provide a different kind of kick and a slightly verdant hue.

⅔ cup green hot pepper sauce (such as green Tabasco)
¼ cup fresh lemon juice
2 tablespoons vegetable oil
2 teaspoons chopped garlic
1 teaspoon freshly ground black pepper
12 wings, cut in half at joints, wing tips removed and discarded

Combine the hot pepper sauce, lemon juice, vegetable oil, garlic, and black pepper in a small bowl.

Place the wings in a resealable plastic bag. Pour the mixture over the wings and shake to coat them. Refrigerate the wings for 2 hours or as long as overnight.

Preheat the oven to 400°F. Cover a rimmed baking sheet with foil and spray the foil with nonstick cooking spray. Remove the wings from the marinade and discard the marinade. Place the wings on the baking sheet. Bake for 25 to 30 minutes or until done.

Hands-Down Best Chicken Wings

▶ This recipe comes from my "grill-friend" Elizabeth Karmel, a Tar Heel native who now lives in Chicago. She is the creator of Girls at the Grill and author of *Taming the Flame: Secrets to Hot-and-Quick Grilling and Low-and-Slow BBQ* (Wiley, 2005). Elizabeth makes these wings every month in her Authentic Southern Barbecue class at the Institute of Culinary Education, and everyone in the class says that they are "hands down" the best wings they have ever eaten! The trick is to allow the hot air to rotate around each wing so that they are crisp all over. If you make them on a grill this occurs naturally. If you make them in an oven, you must use a rack fitted into a sheet pan.

2 (6-ounce) bottles
   Louisiana brand hot
   sauce or Trappey's
   brand hot sauce
   (see Notes)
4 pounds chicken wings
   and/or drumettes
Fine-grain sea salt
Olive oil (optional)

Empty one bottle of the hot sauce into one of two reclosable plastic bags and repeat with the other bag. Divide chicken equally between the two bags. Seal the bags. Turn the chicken occasionally to make sure all surface areas are covered with hot sauce and marinate in the refrigerator for 2 hours or as long as overnight.

When ready to cook, prepare a gas or charcoal grill for indirect heat. Remove the wings from the marinade, discard the marinade, and place the wings in the center of the cooking grate. Close the lid to the grill and let the wings grill for 20 to 25 minutes or until they are beginning to brown. Turn over and continue cooking for another 20 minutes or until the wings are crispy and completely cooked through. Remove from the grill, place on a clean platter, and sprinkle with sea salt. You may want to brush the wings lightly with olive oil to give them a glossy sheen, but this is optional, as wings have enough natural fat in them to keep them moist.

Serve alone with cold beer or with the traditional sides of celery and blue cheese dip.

Notes: Louisiana brand hot sauce, much milder than Tabasco, is distributed nationally, but if you can't find it, use 1 small bottle of Tabasco combined with $1/2$ cup white vinegar and 3 cups water or more to taste.

If you find yourself in a place without a grill and want to make these, preheat your oven to 400°F (if your oven runs hot, reduce the temperature to 375°F) and place the wings on a sheet pan fitted with a rack. Roast the wings in the oven for 20 to 25 minutes, take them out, and turn them over with a pair of tongs. Place the pan back in the oven and continue cooking until golden brown and cooked through. Sprinkle with salt and brush lightly with olive oil if desired.

Mole Olé

▶ This deeply colored rub was inspired by the mole sauces of Mexico, which typically include a variety of roasted peppers and, yes, chocolate. This simpler version uses dried spices and cocoa powder.

½ cup chili powder
2 teaspoons cocoa
1 teaspoon salt
½ teaspoon ground cinnamon
½ teaspoon cayenne pepper
½ teaspoon freshly ground black pepper
½ teaspoon ground cumin
½ teaspoon garlic powder
12 wings, cut in half at joints, wing tips removed and discarded
¼ cup olive oil

In a small bowl, combine the chili powder, cocoa, salt, cinnamon, cayenne, black pepper, cumin, and garlic powder.

Place the wings in a resealable plastic bag. Pour in the olive oil and shake to coat the wings. Pour in the rub mix and shake again to coat the wings. Let sit for 15 to 20 minutes.

Preheat the oven to 400°F. Cover a rimmed baking sheet with foil and spray the foil with nonstick cooking spray. Place the wings on the baking sheet and cook for 20 to 25 minutes or until done, turning the wings about halfway through the cooking time.

Wings with Jim's Fire and Spice Rub

▶ My friend Jim Crabtree in Raleigh, North Carolina, is a master of the grill. He has been tweaking this rub for years. Wear disposable latex gloves when handling the fiery scotch bonnet and the rub containing it. Let's keep this one on the grill, folks.

3 to 4 cloves garlic, chopped
1 fresh scotch bonnet pepper, seeds and veins removed, crushed
4 tablespoons ground allspice
2 tablespoons light brown sugar
2 tablespoons soy sauce (optional)
1 tablespoon vegetable oil
1 tablespoon dried thyme
1 tablespoon paprika
1 teaspoon onion powder
1 teaspoon salt
1 teaspoon ground cinnamon
1 teaspoon ground nutmeg
¼ teaspoon freshly ground black pepper
12 wings, cut in half at joints, wing tips removed and discarded

In a bowl, combine the garlic, scotch bonnet pepper, allspice, brown sugar, soy sauce, if using, oil, thyme, paprika, onion powder, salt, cinnamon, nutmeg, and pepper. Stir and mash to form a paste.

Rub the wings thoroughly with the paste. Cover and refrigerate overnight.

Prepare a gas or charcoal grill for direct cooking. Grill, turning frequently, for 15 to 20 minutes or until done.

Vindaloo Vipers

▶ Shopping at my local Indian market is like taking a journey through a cooking wonderland. On one trip, I found a jar of vindaloo curry paste, which quickly turned a batch of wings into a feast of flame. If you cook these on the grill, turn them frequently to prevent burning.

1 cup vindaloo curry paste

2 tablespoons apple cider vinegar

12 wings, cut in half at joints, wing tips removed and discarded

In a small bowl, stir together the vindaloo curry paste and vinegar. Place the wings in a resealable plastic bag. Pour in the curry mixture and shake to cover the wings. Refrigerate for 2 hours or as long as overnight.

Preheat the oven to 400°F. Cover a rimmed baking sheet with foil and spray the foil with nonstick cooking spray. Remove the wings from the marinade, letting the marinade drip off, and place the wings on the baking sheet. Discard the marinade. Roast for 20 minutes or until done.

Sizzling Szechuan Rubbed Wings

▶ One of my tasters said, "I'm not really a fan of hot food, but these sizzling wings have won me over!" And it's easy to start this fire—you can even prepare the rub a week or two ahead and store it in an airtight jar.

¼ cup chili powder
4 teaspoons ground ginger
1½ teaspoons cayenne pepper
1 teaspoon salt
12 wings, cut in half at joints, wing tips removed and discarded

Preheat the oven to 400°F. Cover a rimmed baking sheet with foil and spray the foil with nonstick cooking spray.

In a small bowl, combine the chili powder, ground ginger, cayenne, and salt. Rub the wings with the mixture and place them on the baking sheet. Let the wings sit for 15 minutes.

Bake the wings for 20 minutes or until done.

Blazin' Cajuns

▶ This easy recipe will make hungry sports fans dance the Cajun two-step. Use a low-salt or salt-free Cajun seasoning, if you can find it.

¾ cup hot sauce (such as
　Tabasco or Crystal)
2 tablespoons vegetable
　oil
2 tablespoons fresh lemon
　juice
2 tablespoons chopped
　garlic
¼ teaspoon salt
12 wings, cut in half
　at joints, wing tips
　removed and discarded
2 tablespoons low-salt
　or salt-free Cajun
　seasoning mix

In a small bowl, stir together the hot sauce, vegetable oil, lemon juice, garlic, and salt. Place the wings in a resealable plastic bag. Pour in the hot sauce mixture and shake to cover the wings. Refrigerate for 2 hours or as long as overnight.

Preheat the oven to 400°F. Cover a rimmed baking sheet with foil and spray the foil with nonstick cooking spray. Remove the wings from the marinade, letting the marinade drip off, and put the wings in a bowl. Discard the marinade. Sprinkle the Cajun seasoning over the wings and toss to coat.

Place the wings on the baking sheet. Roast for 20 to 30 minutes or until done.

Wings with Jumping Jalapeño Sauce

▶ In the South, we love the sweet heat of jalapeño jelly and the crunch of cornmeal. The heat level of these easy-to-make wings will depend on the kind of jalapeño jelly you purchase. If you want to up the ante, add cayenne pepper to the coating.

1 cup yellow cornmeal
1½ teaspoons garlic powder
1¼ teaspoons salt
1 teaspoon onion powder
½ teaspoon freshly ground black pepper
½ teaspoon cayenne pepper, or to taste (optional)
⅓ cup olive oil
12 wings, cut in half at joints, wing tips removed and discarded
1 (10.5-ounce) jar hot jalapeño jelly

Preheat the oven to 400°F. Cover a rimmed baking sheet with foil and spray the foil with nonstick cooking spray.

In a small bowl, combine the cornmeal, garlic powder, salt, onion powder, black pepper, and cayenne, if using. Pour the olive oil into another bowl. Dip the wings lightly in the olive oil, let the excess drip off, then roll the wings in the cornmeal mixture. Place the wings on the baking sheet. Bake for 20 to 30 minutes, or until done.

Meanwhile, put the jalapeño jelly in a saucepan. Heat the jelly over medium-low heat, stirring, until it is melted. Keep it warm until the wings are ready.

While the wings are still warm, place them in a large bowl. Pour the melted jelly over them and toss to coat. Serve warm.

Wings with Fiery Fruit Glaze

▶ My tasters liked the sweet, sour, and spicy combination in this recipe. Be sure to serve these wings warm, and add more habanero, if you dare!

2 cups pineapple juice
2 tablespoons plus 2
   teaspoons white wine
   vinegar
2 tablespoons sugar
1 tablespoon plus 1
   teaspoon vegetable oil
1 tablespoon plus 1
   teaspoon chopped
   garlic
1 tablespoon hot pepper
   sauce (such as Tabasco)
1 teaspoon salt
1 teaspoon freshly ground
   black pepper
12 wings, cut in half
   at joints, wing tips
   removed and discarded
1 (12-ounce) jar peach
   jam
1 habanero, finely
   chopped, or more to
   taste

In a bowl, combine the pineapple juice, vinegar, sugar, vegetable oil, garlic, hot pepper sauce, salt, and pepper. Stir to dissolve the sugar.

Place the wings in a resealable plastic bag. Pour in the pineapple mixture and shake to cover the wings. Refrigerate for 2 hours or as long as overnight.

Place the jam and the habanero in a small saucepan over medium-low heat. Heat, stirring, until the jam is melted. Keep warm over low heat while cooking the wings.

Prepare a gas or charcoal grill for direct cooking. Remove the wings from the marinade and discard the marinade.

continues on p. 80

Grill the wings, turning frequently, for 15 to 20 minutes or until done.

While still warm, place the wings in a large bowl and pour the warm glaze over them. Toss to coat all the wings with the glaze.

FLY HIGH

Jingle Wings

▶ Amuse the kids and astonish your family by shaking up the holiday menu with these super-sized turkey wings. With cranberry and orange juice, they still incorporate traditional flavors. Look for pomegranate molasses at Middle Eastern markets.

1 quart cranberry juice
1 cup orange juice
2 tablespoons vegetable oil
1 tablespoon pomegranate molasses
2 teaspoons grated orange peel
2 teaspoons grated fresh ginger
1 teaspoon salt
4 turkey wings, cut in half at joints, wing tips removed and discarded

GLAZE:
4 tablespoons pomegranate molasses
1 tablespoon honey
1 teaspoon orange juice

In a large bowl, combine the cranberry juice, 1 cup orange juice, oil, pomegranate molasses, orange peel, ginger, and salt. Pour into a large reclosable plastic bag. Add the wings and turn to coat. Refrigerate for 8 to 12 hours.

Preheat the oven to 350°F. Cover a rimmed baking sheet with foil and spray foil with nonstick spray.

Remove the wings from the marinade and discard the marinade. Place the wings on the baking sheet and bake for 30 minutes, turn over, and bake for 15 to 30 minutes more, or until done.

Combine the glaze ingredients in a small bowl and brush on the wings. Bake for 5 to 6 minutes, or until the glaze browns but does not burn.

Hoisin Honeys

▶ Chinese hoisin sauce touched with a little sweetness makes a great marinade for these roasted wings. If you like flavor, you'll love these. If grilling, take care in basting; the sweet sauce may burn.

⅓ cup hoisin sauce
2 tablespoons orange juice
½ teaspoon chopped fresh ginger
½ teaspoon chopped garlic
½ teaspoon honey
¼ teaspoon cayenne pepper
12 wings, cut in half at joints, wing tips removed and discarded

In a small bowl, stir together the hoisin sauce, orange juice, ginger, garlic, honey, and cayenne. Set aside 3 tablespoons of the sauce.

Place the wings in a large reclosable plastic zipper bag. Pour the remaining sauce in over wings and coat them well. Refrigerate the wings in the marinade for 2 to 3 hours.

Preheat the oven to 350°F. Cover a rimmed baking sheet with foil and spray the foil with nonstick cooking spray.

Remove the wings from the marinade and discard the marinade. Place the wings on the baking sheet.

Roast the wings for 25 minutes. Brush the wings with the reserved sauce and bake another 5 minutes or until the wings are done.

Rosemary-Garlic-Lemon Roasters

▶ These wings lend an elegant touch to the pre-game spread. Be sure to finely chop the fresh rosemary so that no one will bite down on large pieces of the herb. Avoid the grill or use lower, indirect heat or the herb coating may burn.

12 wings, cut in half at joints, wing tips removed and discarded
1 cup fresh lemon juice
4 cloves garlic, pressed
2 teaspoons Worcestershire sauce
⅔ cup olive oil
6 tablespoons finely chopped fresh rosemary
1 teaspoon salt
1 teaspoon freshly ground pepper

Place the wings in a reclosable plastic bag. In a small bowl, combine the lemon juice, garlic, and Worcestershire sauce. Pour this mixture into the bag with the wings and refrigerate for 8 hours or overnight.

Preheat the oven to 350°F. Cover a rimmed baking sheet with foil and spray the foil with nonstick cooking spray.

Remove the wings from the marinade and pat dry. Place the olive oil in a small bowl. Dip the wings lightly in the olive oil, let any excess drain off, then place the wings on the baking sheet. Combine the rosemary, salt, and pepper in a small bowl. Sprinkle the rosemary combination on the wings.

Bake the wings for 20 to 30 minutes or until done.

Grilled Chicken Wings Amogio

▶ My good friends, their royal highnesses the BBQ Queens— alias Judith Fertig and Karen Adler—use an Italian marinade to give flavor and punch to their grilled wings. Hope you're a garlic fan! If you use a perforated grill pan, be sure to preheat it along with the grill. And keep these wings outdoors or risk the wrath of the queens! This is from their book *The BBQ Queens' Big Book of Barbecue* (Harvard Common, 2005).

½ cup olive oil

½ cup dry white wine

½ cup fresh lemon juice

¼ cup chopped fresh Italian parsley

3 tablespoons minced garlic

1 tablespoon chopped fresh mint

¼ teaspoon red pepper flakes

3 pounds wings, cut in half at joints, wing tips removed and discarded

Combine the olive oil, white wine, lemon juice, chopped parsley, garlic, mint, and red pepper flakes. Reserve ½ cup of the mixture in a covered container in the refrigerator.

Place the remaining mixture and the wings in a large, resealable plastic bag. Marinate for at least 1 hour or as long as overnight.

Prepare a gas or charcoal grill for direct cooking. Remove the wings from the marinade and discard the marinade. Place the wings on the grill (use a perforated grill pan if the bars on your grill grate are far apart). Cook, turning occasionally, until the wings are nicely browned and crisp all over, about 20 minutes.

To serve, place the wings on a platter and drizzle the reserved mixture over them.

Ginger-Lime Wings with Rum Glaze

▶ Sweet with some heat, these wings have layers of flavor. They're elegant and flavorful enough to hold their own on a fancy buffet or with a light lunch.

½ cup fresh lime juice
2 teaspoons fresh lemon juice
2 teaspoons grated fresh ginger
½ teaspoon salt
½ teaspoon freshly ground black pepper
¼ teaspoon ground nutmeg
12 wings, cut in half at joints, wing tips removed and discarded
¾ cup gold or dark rum
1 tablespoon molasses
½ teaspoon finely chopped garlic
½ of a fresh jalapeño, seeded and finely chopped
2 teaspoons honey

In a bowl, stir together the lime juice, lemon juice, ginger, salt, pepper, and nutmeg.

Place the wings in a resealable plastic bag. Pour the ginger mixture over the wings and let sit for 30 minutes at room temperature or 2 hours in the refrigerator.

In a medium saucepan, stir together the rum, molasses, garlic, and jalapeño, plus 1 cup of water. Bring to a boil, then reduce the heat to medium and simmer, stirring occasionally, until the mixture reduces by about half and forms a glaze, 8 to 10 minutes.

Remove the pan from the heat and stir in the honey. Set aside.

Prepare a gas or charcoal grill for direct cooking.

continues on p. 90

Remove the wings from the marinade and discard the marinade. Place the wings on the grill and cook, turning frequently, for 15 to 20 minutes or until done.

While the wings are still warm, toss them with the glaze.

Wings
Go Coconutty

▶ Crispy and slightly sweet, these wings were inspired by the popular coconut-crusted shrimp. Be sure to get unsweetened coconut, and use a medium-finely to finely shredded kind. These wings are best served immediately after cooking.

2 cups unsweetened
   shredded coconut
2¼ cups all-purpose flour
2 teaspoons paprika
1 teaspoon garlic powder
½ teaspoon onion
   powder
¼ teaspoon salt
1 cup beer
2 large eggs
1½ teaspoons cayenne
   pepper
Vegetable oil for frying
12 wings, cut in half
   at joints, wing tips
   removed and discarded
Hoppin' Hot Honey
   Mustard or Horsey
   Peach Sauce (pages 106
   and 104)

Pour the shredded coconut onto a shallow plate; set aside.

In a bowl, combine 1 cup of the flour, the paprika, garlic powder, onion powder, and salt, and set aside.

In another bowl, combine the beer, eggs, cayenne, and the remaining 1¼ cups of flour. Whisk lightly until no lumps appear, but do not beat.

Pour enough vegetable oil into a heavy frying pan or electric frying pan to reach a depth of about 1½ inches. Heat the oil to 350°F.

Line up your work station thusly: first wings, then garlic powder mixture, beer mixture, and coconut. Roll each wing in the garlic powder mixture and shake

continues on p. 93

off any excess, then roll in the beer batter, letting all excess drip off. Dredge the wings in the coconut and place in the hot oil. Cook the wings, turning several times to brown all sides, for about 15 minutes or until done.

Drain the wings on a wire rack placed over a plate. Serve warm with Hoppin' Hot Honey Mustard or Horsey Peach Sauce.

Pepper-Parmesan Roasters

▶ The flavor of black pepper balances the richness of the Parmesan cheese in this easy yet elegant recipe. These wings are roasted on moderate heat to prevent the cheese from burning. Use indirect or low heat if cooking them on the grill, and turn often.

½ cup grated Parmesan
  cheese
1 tablespoon plus
  1 teaspoon freshly
  ground black pepper
1 teaspoon garlic powder
1 teaspoon salt
12 wings, cut in half
  at joints, wing tips
  removed and discarded

Preheat the oven to 350°F. Cover a rimmed baking sheet with foil and spray the foil with nonstick cooking spray.

In a small bowl, combine the Parmesan, black pepper, garlic powder, and salt.

Place the wings in a reclosable plastic bag. Pour in the pepper mixture, close the bag, and shake to coat the wings.

Remove the wings from the mixture, shaking to remove any excess, and place on the baking sheet. Roast the wings for about 45 minutes, or until done. Turn the wings over 2 or 3 times during cooking so that they will brown evenly.

Margarita on the Wing

▶ These tequila-marinated goodies will transport you straight to the Caribbean. If you prefer a more crispy texture, prepare them on the grill instead of roasting them.

¾ cup fresh lime juice
½ cup tequila
¼ cup vegetable oil
2 tablespoons sugar
2 teaspoons chopped garlic
1 teaspoon grated lime zest
1 teaspoon crushed red pepper flakes
1 teaspoon salt
12 wings, cut in half at joints, wing tips removed and discarded

In a bowl, combine the lime juice, tequila, oil, sugar, garlic, lime zest, red pepper flakes, and salt. Stir to dissolve the salt and sugar.

Place the wings in a reclosable plastic bag. Pour in the lime juice mixture to cover the wings. Refrigerate for at least 2 hours or as long as overnight.

Preheat the oven to 400°F. Cover a rimmed baking sheet with foil and spray the foil with nonstick cooking spray.

Remove the wings from the marinade and discard the marinade. Place the wings on the baking sheet and cook for 25 to 30 minutes, or until the wings are done.

Ooh La La Wings

▶ The fragrant herb blend herbes de Provence is a favorite in French cooking. It's usually a mixture of marjoram, basil, thyme, summer savory, rosemary, fennel seed, sage, and lavender. The flavor takes simple wings to a gourmet level, making them perfect for brunch or a light lunch with a salad. Keep these off the grill; the herbs may burn.

1 cup fresh lemon juice
¼ cup olive oil
2 teaspoons chopped
    garlic
½ teaspoon salt
½ teaspoon freshly
    ground black pepper
12 wings, cut in half
    at joints, wing tips
    removed and discarded
⅔ cup herbes de Provence

In a bowl, combine the lemon juice, olive oil, garlic, salt, and pepper. Place the wings in a reclosable plastic bag. Pour the lemon juice mixture into the bag and shake to coat the wings. Refrigerate for at least 2 hours or as long as overnight.

Preheat the oven to 350°F. Cover a rimmed baking sheet with foil and spray the foil with nonstick cooking spray.

Place the herbes de Provence in a shallow plate and lightly crush the herbs with your fingers, to break up any large whole herbs. Remove the wings from the marinade and discard the marinade. Lightly roll each wing in the herbes de Provence. Do not coat the wings heavily. Place the wings on the baking sheet.

Bake for 30 to 40 minutes or until done.

Roasted Black Pepper Wings with Maple-Bourbon Glaze

▶ The bite of the black pepper contrasts with the sweetness of the maple syrup and bourbon to create a wing with flavor that doesn't stop. Avoid the grill or watch the wings carefully to avoid burning.

2½ tablespoons freshly ground black pepper
1½ teaspoons salt
⅛ teaspoon cayenne pepper
12 wings, cut in half at joints, wing tips removed and discarded

GLAZE:
1 cup bourbon
3 tablespoons maple syrup
2 teaspoons molasses

In a small bowl, combine the black pepper, salt, and cayenne. Place the wings in a reclosable plastic bag. Pour the pepper mixture in the bag, close it, and shake to coat the wings.

Preheat the oven to 350°F. Cover a rimmed baking sheet with foil and spray the foil with nonstick cooking spray. Place the wings on the baking sheet and cook 30 to 40 minutes, or until done.

In a small saucepan over medium heat, combine the bourbon, maple syrup, and molasses, plus 1 cup of water.

continues on p. 100

Bring to a boil, then reduce the heat to simmer. Simmer the mixture until reduced by about half and thickened, 5 to 6 minutes.

When the wings are done, toss them with the glaze while they are still warm.

Piña Colada Coolers

▶ These sweet, mild wings can provide just the right contrast to fiery fliers on your game-day buffet. We must have pity on those with tender tongues. And it's no loss when the flavors are as great as these.

1 cup pineapple juice
½ cup fresh lime juice
2 tablespoons sugar
4 teaspoons vegetable oil
2 teaspoons coconut milk
2 teaspoons dark or gold
   rum
¼ teaspoon ground
   nutmeg
12 wings, cut in half
   at joints, wing tips
   removed and discarded

In a bowl, combine the pineapple juice, lime juice, sugar, oil, coconut milk, rum, and nutmeg. Whisk with a fork to combine and dissolve the sugar.

Put the wings in a resealable plastic bag. Pour in the pineapple mixture. Refrigerate for at least 2 hours or as long as overnight.

Preheat the oven to 400°F. Cover a rimmed baking sheet with foil and spray the foil with nonstick cooking spray. Remove the wings from the marinade and discard the marinade. Place the wings on the baking sheet and cook for 20 to 25 minutes or until done.

Dean's Asian Barbecued Chicken Wings

▶ My foodie friend Dean McCord in Raleigh, North Carolina, frequently prepares these wings for his family, which means they have a kid-friendly seal of approval. He says the recipe comes from a very old cookbook called *The Frog Commissary Cookbook* (Doubleday, 1985), but he usually cooks the wings a bit longer than specified. Below is Dean's version.

⅔ cup hoisin sauce
½ cup light brown sugar
½ cup soy sauce
½ cup ketchup
¼ cup Chinese fermented
    black beans
¼ cup sesame oil
¼ cup rice vinegar
¼ cup molasses
¼ cup prepared
    horseradish
¼ cup Dijon mustard
1 tablespoon minced
    garlic
4 pounds chicken wings

Combine the hoisin sauce, brown sugar, soy sauce, ketchup, black beans, sesame oil, rice vinegar, molasses, horseradish, Dijon mustard, and garlic. Toss the mixture with the wings and refrigerate at least 6 hours or overnight.

Preheat the oven to 400°F. Arrange the wings, with their sauce, in a single layer on foil-lined rimmed baking sheets. Bake for 1 hour, occasionally spooning the sauce on the baking sheets over the wings, until well glazed and a deep reddish brown color.

Bloody Mary Chicks

▶ Plenty of Bloody Marys have been consumed with wings, so why not combine the two? Add more hot sauce and horseradish if you like it spicy.

1 cup tomato-vegetable
  juice
¼ cup fresh lime juice
4 teaspoons
  Worcestershire sauce
4 teaspoons vodka
1½ teaspoons prepared
  horseradish
1 teaspoon celery seed
1 teaspoon hot pepper
  sauce (such as Tabasco)
12 wings, cut in half
  at joints, wing tips
  removed and discarded

In a bowl, combine the tomato-vegetable juice, lime juice, Worcestershire sauce, vodka, horseradish, celery seed, and hot pepper sauce.

Place the wings in a resealable plastic bag. Pour in the vegetable juice mixture and shake to coat the wings. Refrigerate for at least 2 hours or as long as overnight.

Preheat the oven to 400°F. Cover a rimmed baking sheet with foil and spray the foil with nonstick cooking spray. Remove the wings from the marinade and discard the marinade. Place the wings on the baking sheet and cook for 20 to 25 minutes or until done.

Honey-Mustard-Pecan Wings

▶ Here in the South, we love pecans almost as much as we love sports. This recipe combines them with the sweetness of honey and the tang of mustard. Avoid the grill with these, because the nuts may burn. The food processor makes fast work of chopping the pecans.

¼ cup Dijon mustard
¼ cup honey
3 cups chopped pecans
12 wings, cut in half
  at joints, wing tips
  removed and discarded

Preheat the oven to 350°F. Cover a rimmed baking sheet with foil and spray the foil with nonstick cooking spray.

In a bowl large enough to hold the wings, combine the mustard and honey. Add the wings and toss to coat them well. Place the chopped pecans on a plate.

Remove the wings from the honey-mustard mixture and roll in the pecans, pressing lightly so that the nuts will adhere. Place the wings on the baking sheet. Bake for 30 to 45 minutes or until done.

Black Belt Wings

▶ I came up with these wings for a party my husband and I gave for his martial arts class. The group agreed that they're not too hot, but have a great flavor—and go down well with sake.

½ cup orange juice
2 tablespoons soy sauce
1 tablespoon honey
2 teaspoons vegetable oil
1 teaspoon grated fresh
    ginger
1 teaspoon chopped garlic
1 teaspoon Thai chili-
    garlic sauce
1 teaspoon orange liqueur
12 wings, cut in half
    at joints, wing tips
    removed and discarded

In a bowl, combine the orange juice, soy sauce, honey, oil, ginger, garlic, chili-garlic sauce, and orange liqueur. Whisk to blend the ingredients.

Place the wings in a resealable plastic bag. Pour in the orange juice mixture and toss to coat all the wings. Refrigerate for at least 2 hours or as long as overnight.

Preheat the oven to 400°F. Cover a rimmed baking sheet with foil and spray the foil with nonstick cooking spray. Remove the wings from the marinade and discard the marinade. Place the wings on the baking sheet and cook for 20 to 25 minutes or until done.

Crunchy Pretzel Chicken Wings with Chutney-Pecan Dipping Sauce

▶ This recipe was a finalist in the National Chicken Cooking Contest in 1993. The annual contest is sponsored by the National Chicken Council, which offers more great recipes at www.eatchicken.com.

8 tablespoons (1 stick) butter, melted
1 teaspoon cayenne pepper
¼ teaspoon garlic powder
1 cup finely crushed pretzels
½ cup finely chopped pecans
¼ teaspoon freshly ground black pepper
2 pounds broiler-fryer chicken wings, cut in half at joints, wing tips removed and discarded
Chutney-Pecan Dipping Sauce (recipe follows)
Mango slices for garnish

In a shallow bowl, mix together the butter, cayenne, and garlic powder. In another bowl, mix together the pretzels, pecans, and black pepper. Dip each piece of chicken first in the melted butter mixture and then in the pretzel-pecan mixture. Place the wings on a large greased cookie sheet.

Bake in a 350°F oven for about 50 minutes or until a fork can be inserted into the chicken with ease.

Remove the wings from the cookie sheet and place them on a serving dish. Garnish with mango slices. Serve the Chutney-Pecan Dipping Sauce in a separate bowl.

Chutney-Pecan Dipping Sauce

⅓ cup chutney
4 tablespoons butter
¼ cup honey
¼ cup pecan halves

In the container of a food processor or blender, place the chutney, butter, honey, and pecan halves. Process, pulsing on and off, several times, until the pecans are chunky.

Garlic, Glorious Garlic

▶ Fans of "the stinking rose," this one is for you! To speed preparation, purchase already chopped garlic in a jar or use a food processor to chop fresh garlic cloves.

¾ cup chopped garlic
3 tablespoons finely
   chopped onion
1 tablespoon dried thyme,
   crushed
1½ teaspoons olive oil
1½ teaspoons white wine
   vinegar
1½ teaspoons salt
¾ teaspoon dried oregano
¾ teaspoon freshly
   ground black pepper
12 wings, cut in half
   at joints, wing tips
   removed and discarded

In a small bowl, combine the garlic, onion, thyme, oil, vinegar, salt, oregano, and black pepper. Stir and mash until the ingredients are combined and a little like a paste.

Place the wings in a resealable plastic bag. Pour in the garlic mixture and toss to coat the wings. Refrigerate for at least 2 hours or as long as overnight.

Preheat the oven to 400°F. Cover a rimmed baking sheet with foil and spray the foil with nonstick cooking spray. Remove the wings from the marinade and discard the marinade. Bake for 20 to 30 minutes or until done.

Balsamic-Sage Wings

▶ The sweet-sour taste of balsamic vinegar is great on so many things. Pairing it with sage gives a deep flavor to these wings. "Very good, spiced just right," said one of my tasters.

1½ cups balsamic vinegar
⅓ cup olive oil
⅓ cup honey
1 tablespoon chopped garlic
1½ teaspoons salt
1½ teaspoons freshly ground black pepper
1 teaspoon ground sage
12 wings, cut in half at joints, wing tips removed and discarded

In a bowl, whisk together the vinegar, oil, honey, garlic, salt, pepper, and sage. Pour over the wings, cover, and marinate for at least 2 hours or as long as overnight.

Prepare a gas or charcoal grill for direct cooking. Remove the wings from the marinade and discard the marinade. Grill the wings, turning frequently, for 15 to 20 minutes or until done.

Chinese
Five-Spice Chicks

▶ Take your game-time snacks in a new direction with this Asian-inspired combination. Five-spice powder, used in Chinese cooking, usually contains cinnamon, cloves, fennel seed, star anise, and Szechuan pepper. Look for it in larger supermarkets or at Asian markets.

¾ cup vegetable oil
¾ cup white wine vinegar
　or rice wine vinegar
2 tablespoons plus 2
　teaspoons honey
2 tablespoons five-spice
　powder
1 tablespoon sesame oil
1 tablespoon soy sauce
1 tablespoon chopped
　garlic
1 teaspoon salt
12 wings, cut in half
　at joints, wing tips
　removed and discarded

In a bowl, combine the oil, vinegar, honey, five-spice powder, sesame oil, soy sauce, garlic, and salt. Stir well until all ingredients are combined.

Place the wings in a resealable plastic bag. Pour in the oil and vinegar mixture and toss to coat all the wings. Refrigerate at least 2 hours or as long as overnight.

Preheat the oven to 400°F. Cover a rimmed baking sheet with foil and spray the foil with nonstick cooking spray. Remove the wings from the marinade and discard the marinade. Place the wings on the baking sheet and cook for 20 to 25 minutes or until done.

DRESSED TO THRILL

SAUCES, DIPS, SALSAS, AND A FEW SURPRISES

Blue Cheese Dip

▶ The classic hot wing cooler, but gone upscale. This dip's a slam dunk!

1½ cups blue cheese
    crumbles
1 cup mayonnaise
1 cup sour cream
2 cloves garlic, pressed
2 teaspoons Dijon
    mustard
1½ teaspoons freshly
    ground black pepper
½ teaspoon salt

Combine the blue cheese crumbles, mayonnaise, sour cream, garlic, Dijon mustard, pepper, and salt in a large bowl. Using a blender or a stick blender, puree the mixture until fairly smooth. Cover and refrigerate overnight to let the flavors blend.

Horsey Peach Sauce

▶ Sweet and hot—what a great combination. And easy, too. This sauce can be served with any kind of wings, but it is particularly good with Wings Go Coconutty on page 77.

1 cup peach preserves
2 teaspoons prepared
    horseradish

Put the peach preserves and horseradish in a small saucepan over medium-low heat. Stir and heat until slightly melted and combined.

Curry-Chutney Dip

▶ This slightly spicy dip offers an unusual Indian flair to the basic wing. Add more cayenne pepper if you like it hotter.

2 cups plain yogurt
4 teaspoons Major Grey's
   chutney
3 teaspoons curry powder
2 cloves garlic, pressed
1 teaspoon salt
Pinch of cayenne pepper

Combine the yogurt, chutney, curry powder, garlic, salt, and cayenne in a large bowl. Using a blender or a stick blender, puree to remove any large pieces of chutney. Cover and refrigerate overnight to let the flavors blend.

Kiwi-Mango Salsa

▶ This sweet, fruity salsa with the kick of habanero is great on grilled wings.

2 cups chopped kiwifruit
½ cup chopped mango
¼ cup fresh lime juice
1½ teaspoons sugar
1 teaspoon chopped garlic
¼ to ½ teaspoon chopped
   habanero chile
½ teaspoon salt
Freshly ground black
   pepper to taste

Combine the kiwifruit, mango, lime juice, sugar, garlic, habanero, salt, and black pepper in a large bowl. Cover and refrigerate overnight before serving. Drain slightly before serving if the salsa has become too watery.

Hoppin' Hot Honey Mustard

▶ Set those wings on fire with this sweet-spicy sauce. Use it with basic grilled, fried, or roasted wings. It's great with Wings Go Coconutty on page 77. Grainy Creole mustard contains a bit of horseradish.

1 cup Creole mustard
¼ cup plus 2 teaspoons honey
1 teaspoon dry mustard powder
¾ teaspoon cayenne pepper
¼ teaspoon nutmeg

Combine the Creole mustard, honey, dry mustard powder, cayenne, and nutmeg. Serve immediately or cover and refrigerate overnight.

Spicy Taco Sauce

▶ Wings go "olé" with this easy dip. Double the Mexican flavor by using it with the Taco Time Grillers on page 42.

1 cup bottled spicy picante sauce
4 teaspoons chopped fresh cilantro
1 teaspoon chili powder
1 teaspoon fresh lime juice
½ teaspoon cumin
½ teaspoon chopped garlic
¼ teaspoon cayenne pepper

In a large bowl, combine the picante sauce, cilantro, chili powder, lime juice, cumin, garlic, and cayenne. Using a blender or a stick blender, puree the mixture to a smooth consistency. Serve immediately or cover and refrigerate overnight.

Thai Peanut Dipping Sauce

▶ Spicy-hot Thai chili-garlic sauce gives a kick to this dip, which goes well with roasted or grilled wings. Look for the sauce in the Asian section of supermarkets or at Asian markets.

2 teaspoons vegetable oil
2 teaspoons chopped garlic
1 cup creamy peanut butter
⅓ cup soy sauce
2½ teaspoons Thai chili-garlic sauce
4 teaspoons light brown sugar
¼ cup coconut milk
¼ cup chopped fresh cilantro

Heat the vegetable oil in a saucepan over medium heat. Add the garlic and cook, stirring, until softened but not browned, about 2 minutes.

Stir in the peanut butter, soy sauce, chili-garlic sauce, brown sugar, and 2 cups water. Simmer, stirring frequently to prevent sticking, until the mixture thickens, 2 to 4 minutes.

Remove the pan from the heat. Stir in the coconut milk and cilantro. Serve warm.

Wasabi-Horseradish Dip

▶ Who needs bottled dressings when you can whip up this hot and flavorful dip? It will lend its bite to fried, grilled, or roasted wings. Wasabi paste comes in a tube and can be found in Asian markets and larger supermarkets.

1 cup sour cream

2 tablespoons mayonnaise

1 tablespoon plus 1 teaspoon wasabi paste

1 tablespoon prepared horseradish

1 teaspoon ground white pepper

1 teaspoon salt

1 tablespoon chopped fresh parsley or chives

In a bowl, combine the sour cream, mayonnaise, wasabi paste, horseradish, white pepper, and salt. Stir until well mixed. Stir in the parsley or chives. Use immediately or refrigerate, covered, overnight.

Buffalo
Chicken Dip

▶ Shelley Kramer of Raleigh, North Carolina, is a great cook who frequently shares her recipes with me. This party favorite from Shelley takes the flavors of Buffalo wings and turns them into a crowd-pleasing dip. Serve with crackers.

2 to 3 tablespoons
   vegetable oil
½ cup chopped onion
3 (12.5-ounce) cans
   cooked chicken
1 (12-ounce) bottle
   Buffalo wing sauce
2 (8-ounce) packages
   cream cheese
½ cup ranch or blue-
   cheese salad dressing
1 cup chopped celery
2 cups shredded Mexican
   cheese blend

Preheat the oven to 350°F.

In a medium saucepan, heat the oil over medium heat. Add the onion and cook, stirring, until softened, 3 to 5 minutes.

Stir in the chicken, Buffalo wing sauce, cream cheese, salad dressing, and celery. Spread the mixture in a 9- by 13-inch baking dish. Sprinkle the Mexican cheese on top. Bake for 25 to 30 minutes or until the dip is bubbly and the cheese is melted.

Buffalo Wing Bloody Marys

▶ The flavors of that favorite brunch food, Buffalo wings, in the top brunch cocktail, the Bloody Mary. I like to let guests add their own vodka to their individual glasses so that those who prefer a "virgin" drink can enjoy the beverage.

1 quart low-salt pure
   tomato juice
⅓ cup Buffalo wing sauce
2 tablespoons
   Worcestershire sauce
1 tablespoon plus
   2 teaspoons fresh
   lime juice
1 teaspoon freshly ground
   black pepper
Vodka
Lime wedges, for garnish
   (optional)
Celery sticks, for garnish
   (optional)

In a large pitcher, stir together the tomato juice, Buffalo wing sauce, Worcestershire sauce, lime juice, and black pepper. Add vodka to taste. Serve poured over ice in tall glasses, with optional garnishes.

Index